Verse and Prose for Beginners in Reading

Selected from English and American Literature

Verse and Prose for Beginners in Reading

Selected from English and American Literature

Horace Elisha Scudder, editor

PREFACE

The attentive reader of this little book will be apt to notice very soon that though its title is *Verse and Prose for Beginners in Reading*, the verse occupies nine tenths, the prose being confined to about two hundred proverbs and familiar sayings—some of them, indeed, in rhyme—scattered in groups throughout the book. The reason for this will be apparent as soon as one considers the end in view in the preparation of this compilation.

The *Riverside Primer and Reader*, as stated in its Introduction, "is designed to serve as the sole text-book in reading required by a pupil. When he has mastered it he is ready to make the acquaintance of the world's literature in the English tongue." In that book, therefore, the pupil was led by easy exercises to an intelligent reading of pieces of literature, both verse and prose, so that he might become in a slight degree familiar with literature before he parted with his sole text-book. But the largest space had, of necessity, to be given to practice work, which led straight to literature, indeed, though to a small quantity only. The verse offered in that book was drawn from nursery rhymes and from a few of the great masters of poetical form; the prose was furnished by a selection of proverbs, some of the simplest folk stories, and two passages, closing the book, from the Old and New Testaments.

The pupil, upon laying down his *Primer and Reader* and proposing to enter the promised land of literature, could find a volume of prose consisting of *Fables and Folk Stories*, into the pleasures of which he had already been initiated; but until now he could find no volume of poetry especially prepared for him which should fulfill the promise of the verse offered to him in his *Primer and Reader*. Be it remembered that he was not so much to read verse written expressly for him, as to overhear the great poets when they sang so simply, so directly, and yet with so penetrating a note that the burden of their song, full, it may be, to the child's elders, would have an awakening power for the child himself. As so often said, a child can receive and delight in a poem through the ear long before he is able to attain the same pleasure through the eye; and there are many poems in such a book, for example, as Miss Agnes Repplier's *A Book of Famous Verse*, wholly delightful for a child to listen to which yet it would be impossible for him to read to himself.

The agreeable task of the editor, therefore, was to search English and American literature for those poems which had fallen from the lips of poets with so sweet a cadence and in such simple notes that they would offer but slight difficulties to a child who had mastered the rudiments of reading. It was by no means necessary that such poems should have had an audience of children in mind nor have taken childhood for a subject, though it was natural that a few of the verses should prove to be suggested by some aspect of child-life. The selection must be its own advocate, but it may be worth while to point out that the plan of the book supposes an easy approach to the more serious poems by means of the light ditties of the nursery; that there is no more reason for depriving a child of honest fun in his verse than there is for condemning the child's elders to grave poetry exclusively; and that it is not necessary or even desirable for a poem to come at once within the reader's comprehension. To take an extreme case, Tennyson's lines "Break, Break, Break!" would no doubt be ruled out of such a book as this by many in sympathy with children; yet the unexplainable power of the poem is not beyond the apprehension of sensitive natures at an early age.

The contents have been gleaned from a number of sources, and the editor is glad to mingle with the names of the secure dwellers on Parnassus those of some living Americans and Englishmen. He does not pretend that he has made an exhaustive collection, but he hopes the book may be regarded as the nucleus for an anthology which cannot, in the nature of things, be very large.

The prose, as already intimated, is confined to groups of proverbs and familiar sayings. In one aspect these single lines of prose present difficulties to the young reader: they are condensed forms of expression, even though the words may be simple; but they offer the convenient small change of intellectual currency which it is well for one to be supplied with at an early stage of one's journey, and they afford to the teacher a capital opportunity for conversational and other exercises.

The order of this book is in a general way from the easy to the more difficult, with an attempt, also, at an agreeable variety. The editor has purposely avoided breaking up the book into lesson portions or giving it the air of a text-book. There is no reason why children should not read books as older people read them, for pleasure, and dissociate them from a too persistent notion of tasks. It is entirely possible that some teachers may find it out of the question to lead their classes straight through this book, but there is nothing to forbid them from judicious skipping, or, what is perhaps more to the point, from helping pupils over a difficult word or phrase when it is encountered; the interest which the child takes will carry him over most hard places. It would be a capital use of the book also if teachers were to draw upon it for poems which their pupils should, in the suggestive phrase, learn by heart. To this purpose the contents are singularly well adapted; for, from the single line proverb to a poem by Wordsworth, there is such a wide range of choice that the teacher need not resort to the questionable device of giving children fragments and bits of verse and prose to commit to memory. One of the greatest services we can do the young mind is to accustom it to the perception of *wholes*, and whether this whole be a lyric or a narrative poem like Evangeline, it is almost equally important that the young reader should learn to hold it as such in his mind. To treat a poem as a mere quarry out of which a particularly smooth stone can be chipped is to misinterpret poetry. A poem is a statue, not a quarry.

H.E.S.

BOSTON, *October*, 1893.

ALPHABET

A was an apple-pie;
B bit it;
C cut it;
D dealt it;
E ate it;
F fought for it;
G got it;
H had it;
J joined it;
K kept it;
L longed for it:
M mourned for it;
N nodded at it;
O opened it;
P peeped into it;
Q quartered it;
R ran for it;
S stole it;
T took it;
V viewed it;
W wanted it;
X, Y, Z, and amperse-and,
All wished for a piece in hand.

A DEWDROP.

Little drop of dew,
Like a gem you are;
I believe that you
Must have been a star.

When the day is bright,
On the grass you lie;
Tell me then, at night
Are you in the sky?

BEES.

Bees don't care about the snow;
I can tell you why that's so:

Once I caught a little bee
Who was much too warm for me!

* * * * *

Baa, baa, black sheep,
Have you any wool?
Yes, marry, have I,
Three bags full;

One for my master,
And one for my dame,
But none for the little boy
Who cries in the lane.

* * * * *

Bless you, bless you, burnie bee;
Say, when will your wedding be?
If it be to-morrow day,
Take your wings and fly away.

* * * * *

Bow, wow, wow,
Whose dog art thou?
Little Tom Tinker's dog,
Bow, wow, wow.

* * * * *

Bye, baby bunting,
Daddy's gone a-hunting,
To get a little rabbit skin
To wrap the baby bunting in.

* * * * *

Star light, star bright,
First star I see to-night;
I wish I may, I wish I might,
Have the wish I wish to-night.

* * * * *

The little moon came out too soon,
And in her fright looked thin and white,
The stars then shone,
And every one
Twinkled and winked and laughed and blinked.
The great sun now rolled forth in might
And drove them all quite out of sight.

TO A HONEY-BEE.

"Busy-body, busy-body,
Always on the wing,
Wait a bit, where you have lit,
And tell me why you sing."

Up, and in the air again,
Flap, flap, flap!
And now she stops, and now she drops
Into the rose's lap.

"Come, just a minute come,
From your rose so red."
Hum, hum, hum, hum—
That was all she said.

"Busy-body, busy-body,
Always light and gay,
It seems to me, for all I see,
Your work is only play."

And now the day is sinking to
The goldenest of eves,

And she doth creep for quiet sleep
Among the lily-leaves.

"Come, just a moment come,
From your snowy bed."
Hum, hum, hum, hum—
That was all she said.

But, the while I mused, I learned
The secret of her way:
Do my part with cheerful heart,
And turn my work to play.

* * * * *

A cat came fiddling out of a barn,
With a pair of bag-pipes under her arm;
She could sing nothing but fiddle-de-dee,
The mouse has married the bumble-bee;
Pipe, cat,—dance, mouse,—
We'll have a wedding at our good house.

* * * * *

A dillar, a dollar,
A ten o'clock scholar,
What makes you come so soon?
You used to come at ten o'clock,
But now you come at noon.

* * * * *

As I was going to St. Ives,
I met a man with seven wives;
Every wife had seven sacks,
Every sack had seven cats,
Every cat had seven kits:
Kits, cats, sacks, and wives,
How many were there going to St. Ives?

* * * * *

As I was going up Pippen Hill,—
Pippen Hill was dirty,—
There I met a pretty miss,
And she dropped me a curtsy.

Little miss, pretty miss,
Blessings light upon you;
If I had half-a-crown a day,
I'd spend it all upon you.

* * * * *

A swarm of bees in May
Is worth a load of hay;
A swarm of bees in June
Is worth a silver spoon;
A swarm of bees in July
Is not worth a fly.

PROVERBS AND POPULAR SAYINGS.

As blind as a bat.
As broad as it is long.
As cross as two sticks.
As dark as pitch.
As dead as a door nail.
As dead as a herring.
As full as an egg is of meat.
As hot as toast.
As like as two peas.
As merry as a cricket.
As plain as the nose on a man's face.
As quiet as a mouse.
As sharp as a razor.
As straight as an arrow.
As sweet as honey.
As true as steel.
As weak as water.

NONSENSE ALPHABET.

A was an ant
Who seldom stood still,
And who made a nice house
In the side of a hill.
Nice little ant!

B was a bat,
Who slept all the day,
And fluttered about
When the sun went away.
Brown little bat!

C was a camel:
You rode on his hump;
And if you fell off,
You came down such a bump!
What a high camel!

D was a duck
With spots on his back,
Who lived in the water,
And always said "Quack!"
Dear little duck!

E was an elephant,
Stately and wise:
He had tusks and a trunk,
And two queer little eyes.
Oh, what funny small eyes!

F was a fish
Who was caught in a net;
But he got out again,
And is quite alive yet.
Lively young fish!

G was a goat
Who was spotted with brown:
When he did not lie still
He walked up and down.
Good little goat!

H was a hat
Which was all on one side;
Its crown was too high,
And its brim was too wide.
Oh, what a hat!

I was some ice
So white and so nice,
But which nobody tasted;
And so it was wasted.
All that good ice!

J was a jug,
So pretty and white,
With fresh water in it
At morning and night.
Nice little jug!

K was a kite
Which flew out of sight,
Above houses so high,
Quite into the sky.
Fly away, kite!
L was a lily,
So white and so sweet!
To see it and smell it
Was quite a nice treat.
Beautiful lily!

M was a man,
Who walked round and round;
And he wore a long coat

That came down to the ground.
Funny old man!

N was a net
Which was thrown In the sea
To catch fish for dinner
For you and for me.
Nice little net!

O was an orange
So yellow and round:
When it fell off the tree,
It fell down to the ground.
Down to the ground!

P was a polly.
All red, blue, and green,—
The most beautiful polly
That ever was seen.
Poor little polly!
Q was a quail
With a very short tail;
And he fed upon corn
In the evening and morn.
Quaint little quail!

R was a rabbit,
Who had a bad habit
Of eating the flowers
In gardens and bowers.
Naughty fat rabbit!

S was the sugar-tongs,
Nippity-nee,
To take up the sugar
To put in our tea.
Nippity-nee!

T was a tortoise,
All yellow and black:
He walked slowly away,
And he never came back.
Torty never came back!

U was an urn
All polished and bright,
And full of hot water
At noon and at night.
Useful old urn!

V was a veil
With a border upon it,
And a ribbon to tie it
All round a pink bonnet.
Pretty green veil!

W was a watch,
Where, in letters of gold,
The hour of the day
You might always behold.
Beautiful watch!

Y was a yew,
Which flourished and grew
By a quiet abode
Near the side of a road.
Dark little yew!

Z was a zebra,
All striped white and black;
And if he were tame,
You might ride on his back.
Pretty striped zebra!

THE EGG IN THE NEST.

There was a tree stood in the ground,
The prettiest tree you ever did see;
The tree in the wood, and the wood in the ground,
And the green grass growing all around.

And on this tree there was a limb,
The prettiest limb you ever did see;
The limb on the tree, and the tree in the wood,
The tree in the wood, and the wood in the ground,
And the green grass growing all around.

And on this limb there was a bough,
The prettiest bough you ever did see;
The bough on the limb, and the limb on the tree,
The limb on the tree, and the tree in the wood,
The tree in the wood, and the wood in the ground,
And the green grass growing all around.

Now on this bough there was a nest,
And in this nest there were some eggs,
The prettiest eggs you ever did see;
Eggs in the nest, and the nest on the bough,
The bough on the limb, and the limb on the tree,
The limb on the tree, and the tree in the wood,
The tree in the wood, and the wood in the ground,
And the green grass growing all around,
And the green grass growing all around.

* * * * *

Hey! diddle, diddle,
The cat and the fiddle,
The cow jumped over the moon;
The little dog laughed
To see such sport,
And the dish ran away with the spoon.

* * * * *

Pussy sits beside the fire,
How can she be fair?
In comes the little dog,
"Pussy, are you there?
So, so, dear Mistress Pussy,
Pray tell me how do you do?"
"Thank you, thank you, little dog,
I'm very well just now."

* * * * *

Ding dong bell,
The cat's in the well!
Who put her in?—
Little Johnny Green.
Who pulled her out?—
Big Johnny Stout.
What a naughty boy was that
To drown poor pussy cat,
Who never did him any harm,
But killed the mice in his father's barn!

DAISIES.

At evening when I go to bed
I see the stars shine overhead;
They are the little daisies white
That dot the meadow of the Night.

And often while I'm dreaming so,
Across the sky the Moon will go;
It is a lady, sweet and fair,
Who comes to gather daisies there.

For, when at morning I arise,
There's not a star left in the skies;

She's picked them all and dropped them down
Into the meadows of the town.

SPINNING TOP.

When I spin round without a stop
And keep my balance like the top,
I find that soon the floor will swim
Before my eyes; and then, like him,
I lie all dizzy on the floor
Until I feel like spinning more.

PROVERBS AND POPULAR SAYINGS.

Every dog has its day.
Every horse thinks his own pack heaviest.
Every little helps.
Every man for himself, and God for us all.
Faint heart never won fair lady.
Fair words butter no parsnips.
Fine feathers make fine birds.
Follow the river and you will get to the sea.
Fools build houses, and wise men live in them.
For every evil under the sun, there is a remedy, or there is none;
If there be one, try and find It; if there be none, never mind it.
For want of a nail the shoe is lost; for want of a shoe the horse is lost;
for want of a horse the rider is lost.

* * * * *

Bobby Shafto's gone to sea,
With silver buckles at his knee;
He'll come back and marry me,—
Pretty Bobby Shafto!

Bobby Shafto's fat and fair,
Combing out his yellow hair,
He's my love for evermore,—
Pretty Bobby Shafto!

* * * * *

Every lady in this land
Has twenty nails upon each hand
Five and twenty on hands and feet.
All this is true without deceit.

* * * * *

Great A, little a,
Bouncing B!
The cat's in the cupboard,
And she can't see.

* * * * *

Hark, hark,
The dogs do bark,
The beggars are coming to town;
Some in rags,
Some in jags,
And some in velvet gowns.

* * * * *

Sing a song of sixpence,
A pocket full of rye;
Four and twenty blackbirds
Baked in a pie;
When the pie was opened,
The birds began to sing;
Was not that a dainty dish
To set before the king?

The king was in the parlor,
Counting out his money;

The queen was in the kitchen,
Eating bread and honey;

The maid was in the garden,
Hanging out the clothes;
There came a little blackbird,
And snipped off her nose.

Jenny was so mad,
She didn't know what to do;
She put her finger in her ear,
And cracked it right in two.

* * * * *

Hickory, dickory, dock,
The mouse ran up the clock,
The clock struck one,
The mouse ran down;
Hickory, dickory, dock.

* * * * *

Hot-cross buns!
Hot-cross buns!
One a penny, two a penny.
Hot-cross buns!
Hot-cross buns!
Hot-cross buns!
If ye have no daughters,
Give them to your sons.

* * * * *

How does my lady's garden grow?
How does my lady's garden grow?
With cockle shells, and silver bells,
And pretty maids all of a row.

* * * * *

Humpty Dumpty sat on a wall,
Humpty Dumpty had a great fall;
Threescore men and threescore more
Cannot place Humpty Dumpty as he was before.

* * * * *

Hush-a-bye, baby, on the tree-top,
When the wind blows, the cradle will rock,
When the bough bends, the cradle will fall,
Down will come baby, bough, cradle, and all.

* * * * *

Some little mice sat in a barn to spin;
Pussy came by, and popped her head in;
"Shall I come in, and cut your threads off?"
"Oh, no, kind sir, you would snap our heads off."

* * * * *

If all the world were apple-pie?
And all the sea were ink.
And all the trees were bread and cheese,
What should we have for drink?

* * * * *

If wishes were horses,
Beggars might ride;
If turnips were watches,
I would wear one by my side.

* * * * *

I have a little sister, they call her peep, peep;
She wades the waters deep, deep, deep;
She climbs the mountains high, high, high;
Poor little creature, she has but one eye.

WHO STOLE THE BIRD'S NEST?

"To-whit! to-whit! to-whee!
Will you listen to me?
Who stole four eggs I laid,
And the nice nest I made?"

"Not I," said the cow, "Moo-oo!
Such a thing I'd never do.
I gave you a wisp of hay,
But didn't take your nest away.
Not I," said the cow, "Moo-oo!
Such a thing I'd never do."

"To-whit! to-whit! to-whee!
Will you listen to me?
Who stole four eggs I laid,
And the nice nest I made?"

"Bob-o'-link! Bob-o'-link!
Now what do you think?
Who stole a nest away
From the plum-tree, to-day?"

"Not I," said the dog, "Bow-wow!
I wouldn't be so mean, any how!
I gave the hairs the nest to make,
But the nest I did not take.
Not I," said the dog, "Bow-wow!
I'm not so mean, anyhow."

"To-whit! to-whit! to-whee!
Will you listen to me?
Who stole four eggs I laid,
And the nice nest I made?"
"Bob-o'-link! Bob-o'-link!
Now what do you think?
Who stole a nest away
From the plum-tree? to-day?"

"Coo-coo! Coo-coo! Coo-coo!
Let me speak a word, too!
Who stole that pretty nest
From little yellow-breast?"

"Not I," said the sheep; "oh, no!
I wouldn't treat a poor bird so.
I gave wool the nest to line,
But the nest was none of mine.
Baa! Baa!" said the sheep; "oh, no,
I wouldn't treat a poor bird so."

"To-whit! to-whit! to-whee!
Will you listen to me?
Who stole four eggs I laid,
And the nice nest I made?"

"Bob-o'-link! Bob-o'-link!
Now what do you think?
Who stole a nest away
From the plum-tree, to-day?"

"Coo-coo! Coo-coo! Coo-coo!
Let me speak a word, too!
Who stole that pretty nest
From little yellow-breast?"

"Caw! Caw!" cried the crow;
"I should like to know
What thief took away
A bird's nest to-day?"

"Cluck! Cluck!" said the hen;
"Don't ask me again,
Why, I haven't a chick
Would do such a trick.
We all gave her a feather,
And she wove them together.
I'd scorn to intrude
On her and her brood.
Cluck! Cluck!" said the hen,
"Don't ask me again."

"Chirr-a-whirr! Chirr-a-whirr!
All the birds make a stir!
Let us find out his name,
And all cry 'for shame!'"

"I would not rob a bird,"
Said little Mary Green;
"I think I never heard
Of anything so mean."
"It is very cruel, too,"
Said little Alice Neal;
"I wonder if he knew
How sad the bird would feel?"

A little boy hung down his head,
And went and hid behind the bed,
For he stole that pretty nest
From poor little yellow-breast;
And he felt so full of shame,
He didn't like to tell his name.

* * * * *

I saw a ship a-sailing,
A-sailing on the sea;
And oh, it was all laden
With pretty things for thee!

There were comfits in the cabin,
And apples in the hold;
The sails were made of silk,
And the masts were made of gold!

The four and twenty sailors,
That stood between the decks,
Were four and twenty white mice,
With chains about their necks.

The captain was a duck,
With a packet on his back;
And when the ship began to move.
The captain said, "Quack! Quack!"

* * * * *

Jack and Jill went up the hill,
To fetch a pail of water;
Jack fell down, and broke his crown,
And Jill came tumbling after.

* * * * *

Little Bo-peep has lost her sheep,
And can't tell where to find them;
Leave them alone, and they'll come home,
And bring their tails behind them.

Little Bo-peep fell fast asleep,
And dreamed she heard them bleating;

But when she awoke, she found it a joke,
For they were still a-fleeting.

Then up she took her little crook,
Determined for to find them;
She found them indeed, but it made her heart bleed,
For they'd left all their tails behind 'em.

* * * * *

Little boy blue, come blow your horn,
The sheep's in the meadow, the cow's in the corn;
Where's the little boy that tends the sheep?
He's under the haycock, fast asleep.
Go wake him, go wake him. Oh, no, not I;
For if I awake him, he'll certainly cry.

* * * * *

Little girl, little girl, where have you been?
Gathering roses to give to the queen.
Little girl, little girl, what gave she you?
She gave me a diamond as big as my shoe.

* * * * *

Little Jack Horner sat in the corner,
Eating a Christmas pie;
He put in his thumb, and he took out a plum,
And said, "What a good boy am I!"

* * * * *

Little Johnny Pringle had a little pig;
It was very little, so was not very big.
As it was playing beneath the shed,
In half a minute poor Piggie was dead.
So Johnny Pringle he sat down and cried,

And Betty Pringle she lay down and died.
There is the history of one, two, and three,
Johnny Pringle, Betty Pringle, and Piggie Wiggie.

* * * * *

Little Miss Muffet
She sat on a tuffet,
Eating of curds and whey;
There came a black spider,
And sat down beside her,
Which frightened Miss Muffet away.

* * * * *

There was a little man,
And he had a little gun,
And his bullets were made of lead, lead, lead;
He went to the brook.
And he saw a little duck,
And shot it through the head, head, head.
He carried it home
To his wife Joan,
And bade her a fire to make, make, make,
To roast the little duck,
He had shot in the brook,
And he'd go and fetch the drake, drake, drake.

* * * * *

Little Tommy Tucker
Sing for your supper.
What shall I sing?
White bread and butter.

How shall I cut it
Without any knife?

How shall I marry
Without any wife?

PROVERBS AND POPULAR SAYINGS.

At sixes and sevens.
Beauty is but skin deep.
Half a loaf is better than no bread.
Better late than never.
Better live well than long.
Beware of no man more than thyself.
Birds of a feather will flock together.
Christmas comes but once a year;
And when it comes, it brings good cheer;
But when it's gone, it's never the near.
Brag is a good dog, but Holdfast is a better.
By fits and starts.
By and by is easily said.
Care will kill a cat.
Cats hide their claws.
Constant dropping wears the stone.
Count not your chickens before they are hatched.
Debt is the worst poverty.
Do not spur a free horse.
Don't cry till you are out of the wood.
Drive thy business; let not that drive thee.
Early to bed, and early to rise,
Makes a man healthy, wealthy, and wise.
East or west, home is best.
Enough is as good as a feast.
Everybody's business is nobody's business.

HAPPY THOUGHT.

The world is so full of a number of things,
I'm sure we should all be as happy as kings.

THE SUN'S TRAVELS.

The sun is not abed, when I
At night upon my pillow lie;
Still round the earth his way he takes,
And morning after morning makes.

While here at home, in shining day,
We round the sunny garden play,
Each little Indian sleepy-head
Is being kissed and put to bed.

And when at eve I rise from tea,
Day dawns beyond the Atlantic Sea;
And all the children in the West
Are getting up and being dressed.

MY BED IS A BOAT.

My bed is like a little boat;
Nurse helps me in when I embark;
She girds me in my sailor's coat
And starts me in the dark.

At night, I go on board and say
Good-night to all my friends on shore;
I shut my eyes and sail away
And see and hear no more.

And sometimes things to bed I take,
As prudent sailors have to do;
Perhaps a slice of wedding-cake,
Perhaps a toy or two.

All night across the dark we steer;
But when the day returns at last,
Safe in my room, beside the pier,
I find my vessel fast.

THE SWING.

How do you like to go up in a swing,
Up in the air so blue?
Oh, I do think it the pleasantest thing
Ever a child can do!
Up in the air and over the wall,
Till I can see so wide,
Rivers and trees and cattle and all
Over the countryside—

Till I look down on the garden green,
Down on the roof so brown—
Up in the air I go flying again,
Up in the air and down!

* * * * *

Matthew, Mark, Luke, and John
Guard the bed that I lie on!
Four corners to my bed,
Four angels round my head;
One to watch, one to pray,
And two to bear my soul away.

* * * * *

Mistress Mary, quite contrary,
How does your garden grow?
With cockle-shells, and silver bells,
And pretty maids all in a row.

* * * * *

Old King Cole
Was a merry old soul,

And a merry old soul was he;
He called for his pipe,
And he called for his bowl,
And he called for his fiddlers three.
Every fiddler, he had a fiddle,
And a very fine fiddle had he;
Twee tweedle dee, tweedle dee, went the fiddlers.
Oh, there's none so rare,
As can compare
With old King Cole and his fiddlers three!

MOTHER HUBBARD AND HER DOG

Old Mother Hubbard
Went to the cupboard,
To get her poor dog a bone;
But when she came there,
The cupboard was bare,
And so the poor dog had none.

She went to the baker's
To buy him some bread;
But when she came back,
The poor dog was dead.

She went to the joiner's
To buy him a coffin;
But when she came back.
The poor dog was laughing.

She took a clean dish
To get him some tripe;
But when she came back,
He was smoking his pipe.

She went to the fishmonger's
To buy him some fish;

And when she came back,
He was licking the dish.

She went to the ale-house
To get him some beer;
But when she came back,
The dog sat in a chair.

She went to the tavern
For white wine and red;
But when she came back,
The dog stood on his head.

She went to the hatter's
To buy him a hat;
But when she came back,
He was feeding the cat.

She went to the barber's
To buy him a wig;
But when she came back,
He was dancing a jig.

She went to the fruiterer's
To buy him some fruit;
But when she came back,
He was playing the flute.

She went to the tailor's
To buy him a coat;
But when she came back,
He was riding a goat.

She went to the cobbler's
To buy him some shoes;
But when she came back,
He was reading the news.

She went to the seamstress
To buy him some linen;
But when she came back,
The dog was spinning.

She went to the hosiers
To buy him some hose;
But when she came back,
He was dressed in his clothes.

The dame made a curtsy,
The dog made a bow;
The dame said, Your servant,
The dog said; Bow, wow.

RUNAWAY BROOK.

"Stop, stop, pretty water!"
Said Mary one day,
To a frolicsome brook,
That was running away.

"You run on so fast!
I wish you would stay;
My boat and my flowers
You will carry away.

"But I will run after:
Mother says that I may;
For I would know where
You are running away."

So Mary ran on;
But I have heard say,
That she never could find
Where the brook ran away.

BED IN SUMMER.

In winter I get up at night
And dress by yellow candle-light.
In summer, quite the other way,
I have to go to bed by day.

I have to go to bed and see
The birds still hopping on the tree,
Or hear the grown-up people's feet
Still going past me in the street.

And does it not seem hard to you,
When all the sky is clear and blue,
And I should like so much to play,
To have to go to bed by day?

AT THE SEASIDE

When I was down beside the sea
A wooden spade they gave to me
To dig the sandy shore.

My holes were empty like a cup,
In every hole the sea came up,
Till it could come no more.

THE MEETING OF THE SHIPS.

When o'er the silent seas alone,
For days and nights we've cheerless gone,
Oh, they who've felt it know how sweet,
Some sunny morn a sail to meet.

Sparkling at once is ev'ry eye,
"Ship ahoy! ship ahoy!" our joyful cry;

While answering back the sounds we hear,
"Ship ahoy! ship ahoy! what cheer? what cheer?"

Then sails are back'd, we nearer come,
Kind words are said of friends and home;
And soon, too soon, we part with pain,
To sail o'er silent seas again.

PROVERBS AND POPULAR SAYINGS.

A barking dog seldom bites.
A bird in the hand is worth two in the bush.
A cat may look at a king.
A chip of the old block.
A day after the fair.
A fool and his money are soon parted.
A fool may ask more questions in an hour than a wise man can answer
in
seven years.
A fool may make money, but it needs a wise man to spend it.
A friend in need is a friend indeed.
A good garden may have some weeds.
A good workman is known by his chips.
A hard beginning makes a good ending.

* * * * *

Three little kittens lost their mittens,
And they began to cry:
"O mother dear, we very much fear
That we have lost our mittens."

"Lost your mittens, you naughty kittens!
Then you shall have no pie."
"Mee-ow, mee-ow, mee-ow!
And we can have no pie.
Mee-ow, mee-ow, mee-ow!"

* * * * *

Once I saw a little bird
Come hop, hop, hop;
So I cried, "Little bird,
Will you stop, stop, stop?"
And was going to the window
To say, "How do you do?"
But he shook his little tail,
And far away he flew.

* * * * *

One misty, moisty morning,
When cloudy was the weather,
I chanced to meet an old man
Clothed all in leather;
He began to compliment,
And I began to grin,—
"How do you do," and "How do you do,"
And "How do you do" again!

* * * * *

Peter Piper picked a peck of pickled peppers;
A peck of pickled peppers Peter Piper picked;
If Peter Piper picked a peck of pickled peppers,
Where's the peck of pickled peppers Peter Piper picked?

* * * * *

Rid a cock-horse to Banbury-cross
To see an old lady upon a white horse,
Rings on her fingers, and bells on her toes,
And so she makes music wherever she goes.

* * * * *

Three wise men of Gotham
Went to sea in a bowl;
If the bowl had been stronger,
My song would have been longer.

* * * * *

See, saw, sacradown,
Which is the way to London town?
One foot up, the other foot down,
And that is the way to London town.

* * * * *

Simple Simon met a pieman
Going to the fair;
Says Simple Simon to the pieman,
"Let me taste your ware."

Says the pieman to Simple Simon,
"Show me first your penny;"
Says Simple Simon to the pieman,
"Indeed, I have not any."

Simple Simon went a-fishing
For to catch a whale;
All the water he had got
Was in his mother's pail.

Simple Simon went to look
If plums grew on a thistle;
He pricked his fingers very much,
Which made poor Simon whistle.

PRETTY COW.

Thank you? pretty cow, that made
Pleasant milk to soak my bread,
Every day and every night,
Warm, and fresh, and sweet, and white.

Do not chew the hemlock rank,
Growing on the weedy bank;
But the yellow cowslips eat,
That will make it very sweet.
Where the purple violet grows,
Where the bubbling water flows,
Where the grass is fresh and fine.
Pretty cow, go there and dine.

THE STAR.

Twinkle, twinkle, little star;
How I wonder what you are!
Up above the world so high,
Like a diamond in the sky.

When the glorious sun is set,
When the grass with dew is wet,
Then you show your little light,
Twinkle, twinkle, all the night.

In the dark blue sky you keep,
And often through my curtains peep;
For you never shut your eye
Till the sun is in the sky.

As your bright and tiny spark,
Lights the traveller in the dark,
Though I know not what you are,
Twinkle, twinkle, little star.

MARY'S LAMB.

Mary had a little lamb,
Its fleece was white as snow;
And everywhere that Mary went,
The lamb was sure to go.

He followed her to school one day,—
That was against the rule;
It made the children laugh and play,
To see a lamb at school.

So the teacher turned him out,
But still he lingered near,
And waited patiently about,
Till Mary did appear.

Then he ran to her, and laid
His head upon her arm,
As if he said, "I'm not afraid,—
You'll keep me from all harm."

"What makes the lamb love Mary so?"
The eager children cry.
"Oh, Mary loves the lamb, you know,"
The teacher did reply.

PROVERBS AND POPULAR SAYINGS.

A watched pot never boils.

After dinner sit awhile; after supper walk a mile.

All his fingers are thumbs.

All is fish that comes to the net.

All is not gold that glitters.

All's well that ends well.

All work and no play makes Jack a dull boy.

All your geese are swans.

Always taking out of the meal tub, and never putting in, soon comes to the

bottom.

An inch on a man's nose is much.

An old bird is not caught with chaff.

An old dog will learn no new tricks.

As bare as the back of my hand.

* * * * *

Solomon Grundy,
Born on a Monday,
Christened on Tuesday,
Married on Wednesday,
Took ill on Thursday,
Worse on Friday,
Died on Saturday,
Buried on Sunday:
This is the end
Of Solomon Grundy.

* * * * *

The King of France went up the hill,
With twenty thousand men;

The King of France came down the hill,
And ne'er went up again.

* * * * *

The man in the wilderness asked me,
How many strawberries grew in the sea.
I answered him, as I thought good,
As many red herrings as grew in the wood.

* * * * *

There was a crooked man, and he went a crooked mile,
He found a crooked sixpence against a crooked stile:
He bought a crooked cat, which caught a crooked mouse,
And they all lived together in a little crooked house.

* * * * *

Tom, Tom, the piper's son,
Stole a pig and away he run!
The pig was eat, and Tom was beat,
And Tom went roaring down the street.

* * * * *

There was a little boy went into a barn,
And lay down on some hay;
An owl came out and flew about,
And the little boy ran away.

* * * * *

There was a man of our town,
And he was wondrous wise;
He jumped into a bramble bush,
And scratched out both his eyes:
And when he saw his eyes were out,

With all his might and main
He jumped into another bush,
And scratched 'em in again.

* * * * *

1. This pig went to market; 2. This pig stayed at home; 3. This pig had a bit of meat; 4. And this pig had none; 5. This pig said, "Wee, wee, wee! I can't find my way home."

* * * * *

Tom, Tom, of Islington,
Married a wife on Sunday;
Brought her home on Monday;
Hired a house on Tuesday;
Fed her well on Wednesday;
Sick was she on Thursday;
Dead was she on Friday;
Sad was Tom on Saturday,
To bury his wife on Sunday.

WEE WILLIE WINKIE.

Wee Willie Winkie
Runs through the town,
Upstairs and downstairs,
In his night-gown;
Tapping at the window,
Crying at the lock,
"Are the babes in their bed?
For it's now ten o'clock."

SINGING.

Of speckled eggs the birdie sings
And nests among the trees;
The sailor sings of ropes and things
In ships upon the seas.

The children sing in far Japan,
The children sing in Spain;
The organ with the organ man
Is singing in the rain.

THE COW.

The friendly cow all red and white,
I love with all my heart;
She gives me cream with all her might,
To eat with apple-tart.

She wanders lowing here and there,
And yet she cannot stray,
All in the pleasant open air,
The pleasant light of day;

And blown by all the winds that pass
And wet with all the showers.
She walks among the meadow grass
And eats the meadow flowers.

GOOD-NIGHT AND GOOD-MORNING.

A fair little girl sat under a tree,
Sewing as long as her eyes could see;
Then smoothed her work and folded it right
And said, "Dear work, good-night, good-night!"

Such a number of rooks came over her head,
Crying "Caw! Caw!" on their way to bed,
She said, as she watched their curious flight,
"Little black things, good-night, good-night!"

The horses neighed, and the oxen lowed,
The sheep's "Bleat! Bleat!" came over the road;
All seeming to say, with a quiet delight,
"Good little girl, good-night, good-night!"

She did not say to the sun, "Good-night!"
Though she saw him there like a ball of light;
For she knew he had God's time to keep
All over the world and never could sleep.

The tall pink foxglove bowed his head;
The violets curtsied, and went to bed;
And good little Lucy tied up her hair,
And said, on her knees, her favorite prayer.

And while on her pillow she softly lay,
She knew nothing more till again it was day;
And all things said to the beautiful sun,
"Good-morning, good-morning! our work is begun."

MOTHER'S EYES.

What are the songs the mother sings?
Of birds and flowers and pretty things;
Baby lies in her arms and spies
All his world in the mother's eyes.

What are the tales the mother tells?
Of gems and jewels and silver bells;
Baby lies in her arms and spies
All his wealth in the mother's eyes.

What are the thoughts in the mother's mind?
Of the gentle Saviour, loving and kind;
Baby lies in her arms and spies
All his heaven in the mother's eyes.

THE LAND OF NOD.

From breakfast on through all the day
At home among my friends I stay,
But every night I go abroad
Afar into the land of Nod.

All by myself I have to go,
With, none to tell me what to do—
All alone beside the streams
And up the mountain sides of dreams.

The strangest things are there for me,
Both things to eat and things to see,
And many frightening sights abroad,
Till morning in the land of Nod.

Try as I like to find the way,
I never can get back by day,
Nor can remember plain and clear
The curious music that I hear.

PROVERBS AND POPULAR SAYINGS.

A lass that has many wooers oft fares the worst.
A lazy sheep thinks its wool heavy.
A little leak will sink a great ship.
A living dog is better than a dead lion.
A man of words, and not of deeds, is like a garden full of weeds.
A man's house is his castle.
A miss is as good as a mile.
A penny for your thought.
A penny saved is a penny got.
A rolling stone will gather no moss.
A small spark makes a great fire.
A stitch in time saves nine.
A tree is known by its fruit.

* * * * *

When I was a little boy, I lived by myself,
And all the bread and cheese I got I put upon the shelf;
The rats and the mice did lead me such a life,
I was forced to go to London to buy me a wife.

The streets were so broad, and the lanes were so narrow,
I could not get my wife home without a wheelbarrow;
The wheelbarrow broke, my wife got a fall,
Down tumbled wheelbarrow, little wife, and all.

* * * * *

Where are you going, my pretty maid?
"I'm going a-milking, sir," she said.
May I go with you, my pretty maid?
"You're kindly welcome, sir," she said.
What is your father, my pretty maid?
"My father's a farmer, sir," she said.

Say, will you marry me, my pretty maid?
"Yes, if you please, kind sir," she said.
Will you be constant, my pretty maid?
"That I can't promise you, sir," she said.
Then I won't marry you, my pretty maid!
"Nobody asked you, sir!" she said.

* * * * *

Who killed Cock Robin?
"I," said the Sparrow,
"With my bow and arrow,
I killed Cock Robin."

Who saw him die?
"I," said the Fly,
"With my little eye,
And I saw him die."

Who caught his blood?
"I," said the Fish,
"With my little dish,
And I caught his blood."

Who made his shroud?
"I," said the Beadle,
"With my little needle,
And I made his shroud."

Who shall dig his grave?
"I," said the Owl,
"With my spade and showl [shovel],
And I'll dig his grave."

Who'll be the parson?
"I," said the Rook,

"With my little book,
And I'll be the parson"

Who'll be the clerk?
"I," said the Lark,
"If it's not in the dark,
And I'll be the clerk."

Who'll carry him to the grave?
"I," said the Kite,
"If 't is not in the night,
And I'll carry him to his grave."

Who'll carry the link?
"I," said the Linnet,
"I'll fetch it in a minute,
And I'll carry the link."

Who'll be the chief mourner?
"I," said the Dove,
"I mourn for my love,
And I'll be chief mourner."

Who'll bear the pall?
"We," said the Wren,
Both the cock and the hen,
"And we'll bear the pall."

Who'll sing a psalm?
"I," said the Thrush,
As she sat in a bush,
"And I'll sing a psalm."

And who'll toll the bell?
"I," said the Bull,
"Because I can pull;"
And so, Cock Robin, farewell.

EPITAPH FOR ROBIN REDBREAST.

Thou shalt have a little bed
Made for thee, and overspread
With brown leaves for coverlet,
Which the tearful dew has wet.
I, among the songs of Spring,
Will miss the song thou didst not sing.

"PLAY WITH ME!"

The kitten came this morning, and said,
With a touch of her paw and a turn of her head?
"Play, play with me!"

And Skye, the terrier, caught my hand,
And tried to make me understand,—
"Play, play with me!"

And Nelly nipped my shoulder quite hard,
And then she went prancing around the yard—
"Play, play with me!"

I played with them all! Now, wouldn't you play,
If a little child, like me, should say,
"Play, play with me?"

THE PIPER.

Piping down the valleys wild.
Piping songs of pleasant glee,
On a cloud I saw a child,
And he laughing said to me:—

"Pipe a song about a lamb:"
So I piped with merry cheer.

"Piper, pipe that song again:"
So I piped; he wept to hear.

"Drop thy pipe, thy happy pipe,
Sing thy songs of happy cheer:"
So I sung the same again,
While he wept with joy to hear.

"Piper, sit thee down and write
In a book that all may read."
So he vanish'd from my sight;
And I pluck'd a hollow reed,

And I made a rural pen,
And I stain'd the water clear,
And I wrote my happy songs
Every child may joy to hear.

INFANT JOY.

I have no name—
I am but two days old.
What shall I call thee?
I happy am,
Joy is my name.—
Sweet joy befall thee!

Pretty joy!
Sweet joy but two days old.
Sweet joy I call thee,
Thou dost smile,
I sing the while,
Sweet joy befall thee!

THE LAMB.

Little lamb, who made thee?
Dost thou know who made thee,
Gave thee life and bid thee feed
By the stream and o'er the mead;
Gave thee clothing of delight,
Softest cloth, woolly, bright;
Gave thee such a tender voice
Making all the vales rejoice;
Little lamb, who made thee?
Dost thou know who made thee?
Little lamb, I'll tell thee,
Little lamb, I'll tell thee.
He is called by thy name,
For He calls himself a Lamb:
He is meek and he is mild,
He became a little child,
I a child and thou a lamb,
We are called by His name.
Little lamb, God bless thee,
Little lamb, God bless thee.

THE LITTLE BOY LOST.

Father! father! where are you going?
Oh, do not walk so fast.
Speak, father speak to your little boy,
Or else I shall be lost.

The night was dark, no father was there;
The child was wet with dew;
The mire was deep and the child did weep,
And away the vapor flew.

THE LITTLE BOY FOUND.

The little boy lost in the lonely fen,
Led by the wandering light,
Began to cry; but God, ever nigh,
Appeared like his father in white;

He kissed the child, and by the hand led,
And to his mother brought,
Who, in sorrow pale, through the lonely dale,
Her little boy weeping sought.

ON THE VOWELS.

We are little airy creatures,
All of different voice and features;
One of us in glass is set,
One of us you'll find in jet.
T' other you may see in tin,
And the fourth a box within.
If the fifth you should pursue,
It can never fly from you.

LETTERS.

Every day brings a ship,
Every ship brings a word;
Well for those who have no fear,
Looking seaward well assured
That the word the vessel brings
Is the word they wish to hear.

ON A CIRCLE.

I'm up and down, and round about,
Yet all the world can't find me out;
Though hundreds have employed their leisure,
They never yet could find my measure.
I'm found almost in every garden,
Nay, in the compass of a farthing.
There's neither chariot, coach, nor mill,
Can move an inch except I will.

ARIEL'S SONG.

Where the bee sucks, there suck I;
In a cowslip's bell I lie:
There I couch, when owls do cry.
On the bat's back I do fly,
After summer, merrily:
Merrily, merrily, shall I live now
Under the blossom, that hangs on the bough.

PROVERBS AND POPULAR SAYINGS.

Forgive and forget.
Fortune helps them that help themselves.
Give a thief rope enough, and he'll hang himself.
Give him an inch, and he'll take an ell.
Go farther and fare worse.
Good wine needs no bush.
Handsome is that handsome does.
Happy as a king.
Haste makes waste, and waste makes want, and want makes strife between the
good-man and his wife.
He cannot say boo to a goose.
He knows on which side his bread is buttered.

SONG.

There is dew for the floweret,
And honey for the bee,
And bowers for the wild bird,
And love for you and me.

There are tears for the many,
And pleasure for the few;
But let the world pass on, dear,
There's love for me and you.

YOUTH AND AGE.

Impatient of his childhood,
"Ah me!" exclaims young Arthur,
Whilst roving in the wild wood,
"I wish I were my father!"
Meanwhile, to see his Arthur
So skip, and play, and run,
"Ah me!" exclaims the father,
"I wish I were my son!"

UPON SUSANNA'S FEET.

Her pretty feet
Like snails did creep
A little out, and then,
As if they played at bo-peep,
Did soon draw in again.

UPON A CHILD THAT DIED.

Here she lies, a pretty bud,
Lately made of flesh and blood:
Who as soon fell fast asleep,
As her little eyes did peep.
Give her strewings, but not stir
The earth that lightly covers her.

CHERRY-RIPE.

Cherry-ripe, ripe, ripe, I cry,
Full and fair ones; come and buy!
If so be you ask me where
They do grow, I answer, There,
Where my Julia's lips do smile;
There's the land, or cherry-isle,
Whose plantations fully show
All the year where cherries grow.

ANSWER TO A CHILD'S QUESTION.

Do you ask what the birds say? The sparrow, the dove,
The linnet and thrush say, "I love and I love!"
In the winter they're silent—the wind is so strong;
What it says, I don't know; but it sings a loud song.
But green leaves, and blossoms, and sunny warm weather,
And singing, and loving—all come back together,
But the lark is so brimful of gladness and love,
The green fields below him, the blue sky above,
That he sings, and he sings; and forever sings he—
"I love my Love, and my Love loves me!"

PROVERBS AND POPULAR SAYINGS.

He sees an inch afore his nose.
He takes the bull by the horns.
He that fights and runs away may live to fight another day.
He that goes a borrowing, goes a sorrowing.
He that has but four and spends five has no need of a purse.
He that knows not how to hold his tongue knows not how to talk.
He that lives on hope has but a slender diet.
He that plants trees loves others besides himself.
He that will steal a pin will steal a better thing.
He was born with a silver spoon in his mouth.
He's in clover.
His bread is buttered on both sides.
His room is better than his company.
Hunger is the best sauce.
I have other fish to fry.

"ONE, TWO, THREE!"

It was an old, old, old, old lady,
And a boy that was half past three;
And the way that they played together
Was beautiful to see.

She couldn't go running and jumping,
And the boy, no more could he;
For he was a thin little fellow,
With a thin little twisted knee.

They sat in the yellow sunlight,
Out under the maple-tree;
And the game that they played I'll tell you,
Just as it was told to me.

It was Hide-and-Go-Seek they were playing,
Though you'd never have known it to be—
With an old, old, old, old lady,
And a boy with a twisted knee.

The boy would bend his face down
On his one little sound right knee,
And he'd guess where she was hiding,
In guesses One, Two, Three!

"You are in the china-closet!"
He would cry, and laugh with glee—
It wasn't the china-closet;
But he still had Two and Three.

"You are up in Papa's big bedroom,
In the chest with the queer old key!"
And she said: "You are *warm* and *warmer*;
But you're not quite right," said she.

"It can't be the little cupboard
Where Mamma's things used to be—
So it must be the clothes-press, Gran'ma!"
And he found her with his Three.

Then she covered her face with her fingers,
That were wrinkled and white and wee,
And she guessed where the boy was hiding,
With a One and a Two and a Three.

And they never had stirred from their places,
Right under the maple-tree—
This old, old, old, old lady,
And the boy with the lame little knee—
This dear, dear, dear old lady,
And the boy who was half past three.

THE BIRD AND ITS NEST.

What does little birdie say,
In her nest at peep of day?
"Let me fly," says little birdie;
"Mother, let me fly away."
"Birdie, rest a little longer,
Till the little wings are stronger."
So she rests a little longer,
Then she flies away.
What does little baby say
In her bed at peep of day?
Baby says, like little birdie,
"Let me rise and fly away."
"Baby, sleep a little longer,
Till the little limbs are stronger."
If she sleeps a little longer,
Baby, too, shall fly away.

PROVERBS AND POPULAR SAYINGS.

Tell no tales out of school.
The bird that can sing, and won't sing, must be made to sing.
You have put the cart before the horse.
It is the early bird that catches the worm.
There is many a slip 'twixt the cup and the lip.
The more haste, the less speed.
They who make the best use of their time have none to spare.
Those who play with edge tools must expect to be cut.
Three removes are as bad as a fire.
Through thick and thin.
Time and tide wait for no man.
To beat about the bush.
To break the ice.
To buy a pig in a poke.
To find a mare's nest.

WINDY NIGHTS.

Whenever the Moon and stars are set,
Whenever the wind is high,
All night long in the dark and wet,
A man goes riding by.
Late in the night when the fires are out
Why does he gallop and gallop about?

Whenever the trees are crying aloud,
And ships are tossed at sea,
By, on the highway, low and loud,
By, at the gallop goes he.
By, at the gallop he goes, and then
By, he comes back at the gallop again.

NONSENSE VERSES.

There was an Old Man with a nose,
Who said, "If you choose to suppose
That my nose is too long, you are certainly wrong!"
That remarkable Man with a nose.

There was an Old Man on a hill,
Who seldom, if ever, stood still;
He ran up and down in his Grandmother's gown,
Which adorned that Old Man on a hill.

There was an Old Person of Dover,
Who rushed through a field of blue clover;
But some very large Bees stung his nose and his knees,
So he very soon went back to Dover.

There was an Old Man who said, "Hush!
I perceive a young bird in this bush!"
When they said, "Is it small?" he replied, "Not at all;
It is four times as big as the bush!"

There was an Old Man of the West,
Who never could get any rest;
So they set him to spin on his nose and his chin,
Which cured that Old Man of the West.

There was an Old Man who said, "Well!
Will nobody answer this bell?
I have pulled day and night, till my hair has grown white,
But nobody answers this bell!"

There was an Old Man with a beard,
Who said, "It is just as I feared!—
Two Owls and a Hen, four Larks and a Wren,
Have all built their nests in my beard."

There was an Old Person of Dean
Who dined on one pea and one bean;
For he said, "More than that would make me too fat,"
That cautious Old Person of Dean.

There was an Old Man of El Hums,
Who lived upon nothing but crumbs,
Which he picked off the ground, with the other birds round,
In the roads and the lanes of El Hums.

PROVERBS AND POPULAR SAYINGS.

If wishes were horses beggars would ride.
Ill news travels fast.
It never rains but it pours.
It is a long lane that has no turning.
It is an ill wind that blows no man good.
It is easier to pull down than to build.
It is never too late to mend.
Keep thy shop, and thy shop will keep thee.
Leave well enough alone.
Let every tub stand on its own bottom.
Let them laugh that win.
Like father, like son.
Little and often fills the purse.
Look ere you leap.

SONG.

Oh, were my love yon lilac fair,
With purple blossoms to the spring;
And I a bird to shelter there.
When wearied on my little wing!

How I would mourn, when it was torn,
By autumn wild, and winter rude!

But I would sing, on wanton wing,
When youthful May its bloom renewed.

SWEET AND LOW.

Sweet and low, sweet and low,
Wind of the western sea,
Low, low, breathe and blow,
Wind of the western sea!
Over the rolling waters go,
Come from the dying moon, and blow,
Blow him again to me;
While my little one, while my pretty one, sleeps.

Sleep and rest, sleep and rest,
Father will come to thee soon;
Best, rest on mother's breast,
Father will come to thee soon;
Father will come to his babe in the nest,
Silver sails all out of the west
Under the silver moon:
Sleep, my little one, sleep, my pretty one, sleep.

AGAINST IDLENESS AND MISCHIEF.

How doth the little busy bee
Improve each shining hour,
And gather honey all the day
From every opening flower!

How skilfully she builds her cell,
How neat she spreads the wax!
And labors hard to store it well
With the sweet food she makes.

In works of labor or of skill,
I would be busy too;

For Satan finds some mischief still
For idle hands to do.

In books, or work, or healthful play,
Let my first years be past,
That I may give for every day
Some good account at last.

"BREAK, BREAK, BREAK!"

Break, break, break,
On thy cold gray stones, O Sea!
And I would that my tongue could utter
The thoughts that arise in me.

Oh, well for the fisherman's boy,
That he shouts with his sister at play!
Oh, well for the sailor lad,
That he sings in his boat on the bay!

And the stately ships go on
To their haven under the hill;
But oh, for the touch of a vanished hand,
And the sound of a voice that is still!

Break, break, break,
At the foot of thy crags, O Sea!
But the tender grace of a day that is dead
Will never come back to me.

THE ARROW AND THE SONG.

I shot an arrow into the air,
It fell to earth, I knew not where;
For, so swiftly it flew, the sight
Could not follow it in its flight.

I breathed a song into the air,
It fell to earth, I knew not where;
For who has sight so keen and strong,
That it can follow the flight of song?

Long, long afterward, in an oak
I found the arrow, still unbroke;
And the song, from beginning to end,
I found again in the heart of a friend.

PROVERBS AND POPULAR SAYINGS.

Love me little, love me long,
Is the burden of my song.
Many a true word is spoken in jest.
Many hands make light work.
Money is a good servant, but a bad master.
My mind to me a kingdom is.
Never be weary of well doing.
No cross, no crown.
No man can serve two masters.
No news is good news.
No smoke without some fire.
Not worth a pin.
Of two ills choose the least.
One cannot be in two places at once.
One good turn demands another.

THE TABLE AND THE CHAIR.

Said the Table to the Chair,
"You can hardly be aware
How I suffer from the heat
And from chilblains on my feet.
If we took a little walk,
We might have a little talk;
Pray let us take the air,"
Said the Table to the Chair.

Said the Chair unto the Table,
"Now, you know we are not able:
How foolishly you talk,
When you know we cannot walk!"
Said the Table with a sigh,
"It can do no harm to try.
I've as many legs as you:
Why can't we walk on two?"

So they both went slowly down,
And walked about the town
With a cheerful bumpy sound
As they toddled round and round;
And everybody cried,
As they hastened to their side,
"See! the Table and the Chair
Have come out to take the air!"
But in going down an alley,
To a castle in a valley,
They completely lost their way,
And wandered all the day;
Till, to see them safely back,
They paid a Ducky-quack,

And a Beetle, and a Mouse,
Who took them to their house.

Then they whispered to each other.
"O delightful little brother,
What a lovely walk we've taken!
Let us dine on beans and bacon."
So the Ducky and the leetle
Browny-Mousy and the Beetle
Dined, and danced upon their heads
Till they toddled to their beds.

THE OWL.

I.

When cats run home and the light is come
And dew is cold upon the ground,
And the far-off stream is dumb,
And the whirring sail goes round,
And the whirring sail goes round;
Alone and warming his five wits,
The white owl in the belfry sits.

II.

When merry milkmaids click the latch,
And rarely smells the new-mown hay,
And the cock hath sung beneath the thatch
Twice or thrice his roundelay,
Twice or thrice his roundelay;
Alone and warming his five wits,
The white owl in the belfry sits.

THE OWL THE PUSSY-CAT.

The Owl and the Pussy-Cat went to sea
In a beautiful pea-green boat:
They took some honey and plenty of money
Wrapped up In a five-pound note.
The Owl looked up to the stars above,
And sang to a small guitar,
"O lovely Pussy, O Pussy, my love,
What a beautiful Pussy you are,
You are,
You are!
What a beautiful Pussy you are!"

Pussy said to the Owl, "You elegant fowl,
How charmingly sweet you sing!
Oh, let us be married; too long we have tarried:
But what shall we do for a ring?"
They sailed away, for a year and a day,
To the land where the bong-tree grows;
And there in a wood a Piggy-wig stood,
With a ring at the end of his nose,
His nose,
His nose,
With a ring at the end of his nose.

"Dear Pig, are you willing to sell for one shilling
Your ring?" Said the Piggy, "I will."
So they took it away, and were married next day
By the Turkey who lives on the hill.
They dined on mince and slices of quince,
Which they ate with a runcible spoon;
And hand in hand, on the edge of the sand,
They danced by the light of the moon,
The moon,

The moon,
They danced by the light of the moon.

PROVERBS AND POPULAR SAYINGS.

One man's meat is another man's poison.
Out of debt out of danger.
Out of the frying-pan into the fire.
Penny wise and pound foolish.
Riches have wings.
Robin Hood's choice: this or nothing.
Rome was not built in a day.
Save at the spiggot, and lose at the bung.
Second thoughts are best.
Set a thief to take a thief.
A short horse is soon curried.
Take the will for the deed.
Take away my good name, take away my life.
Take time by the forelock.

FABLE.

The mountain and the squirrel
Had a quarrel,
And the former called the latter "Little Prig;"
Bun replied,
"You are doubtless very big;
But all sorts of things and weather
Must be taken in together,
To make up a year
And a sphere.
And I think it no disgrace
To occupy my place.
If I'm not so large as you,
You are not so small as I,
And not half so spry.
I'll not deny you make
A very pretty squirrel track;
Talents differ; all is well and wisely put;
If I cannot carry forests on my back,
Neither can you crack a nut."

WRITTEN IN MARCH

WHILE RESTING ON THE BRIDGE AT THE FOOT OF BROTHER'S WATER.

The Cock is crowing,
The stream is flowing,
The small birds twitter,
The lake doth glitter,
The green field sleeps in the sun;
The oldest and youngest
Are at work with the strongest;
The cattle are grazing.

Their heads never raising;
There are forty feeding like one!

Like an army defeated
The snow hath retreated,
And now doth fare ill
On the top of the bare hill;
The Ploughboy is whooping—anon—anon
There's joy in the mountains;
There's life in the fountains;
Small clouds are sailing,
Blue sky prevailing;
The rain is over and gone!

THOSE EVENING BELLS.

Those evening bells! those evening bells!
How many a tale their music tells,
Of youth, and home, and that sweet time,
When last I heard their soothing chime.

Those joyous hours are passed away;
And many a heart, that then was gay,
Within the tomb now darkly dwells,
And hears no more those evening bells.

And so 't will be when I am gone;
That tuneful peal will still ring on,
While other bards shall walk these dells,
And sing your praise, sweet evening bells.

TO A BUTTERFLY.

I've watched you now a full half hour
Self-poised upon that yellow flower;
And, little Butterfly! indeed
I know not if you sleep or feed.
How motionless!—not frozen seas
More motionless!—and then
What joy awaits you, when the breeze
Hath found you out among the trees,
And calls you forth again!
This plot of orchard-ground is ours;
My trees they are, my Sister's flowers:
Here rest your wings when they are weary,
Here lodge as in a sanctuary!
Come often to us, fear no wrong;
Sit near us on the bough!
We'll talk of sunshine and of song,
And summer days, when we were young;
Sweet childish days, that were as long
As twenty days are now.

PROVERBS AND POPULAR SAYINGS.

To follow one's nose.
To have a finger in the pie.
To hit the nail on the head.
To kill two birds with one stone.
To make a spoon, or spoil a horn.
To pour oil into the fire is not the way to quench it.
Two heads are better than one.
Waste not, want not.
We easily forget our faults when nobody knows them.
We never know the worth of water till the well is dry.
When Adam delved and Eve span, who was then the gentleman?
When the cat is away, the mice will play.
Strike when the iron is hot.
Where there's a will, there's a way.
You cannot eat your cake and have it too.
You must take the fat with the lean.

LUCY.

She dwelt among the untrodden ways
Beside the springs of Dove;
A maid whom there were none to praise,
And very few to love.

A violet by a mossy stone
Half-hidden from the eye!—
Fair as a star, when only one
Is shining in the sky.

She lived unknown, and few could know
When Lucy ceased to be;
But she is in her grave, and oh!
The difference to me.

LUCY GRAY, OR SOLITUDE.

Oft I had heard of Lucy Gray;
And, when I crossed the wild,
I chanced to see, at break of day,
The solitary child.

No mate, no comrade Lucy knew;
She dwelt on a wide moor,—
The sweetest thing that ever grew
Beside a human door!

You yet may spy the fawn at play,
The hare upon the green;
But the sweet face of Lucy Gray
Will nevermore be seen.

"To-night will be a stormy night,—
You to the town must go;
And take a lantern, Child, to light
Your mother through the snow."

"That, Father! will I gladly do:
'T is scarcely afternoon,—
The minster-clock has just struck two,
And yonder is the moon!"

At this the father raised his hook,
And snapped a fagot-band;
He plied his work;—and Lucy took
The lantern in her hand.

Not blither is the mountain roe;
With many a wanton stroke
Her feet disperse the powdery snow,
That rises up like smoke.

The storm came on before its time,
She wandered up and down;
And many a hill did Lucy climb,
But never reached the town.

The wretched parents all that night
Went shouting far and wide;
But there was neither sound nor sight
To serve them for a guide.

At daybreak on the hill they stood
That overlooked the moor;
And thence they saw the bridge of wood,
A furlong from their door.

They wept—and, turning homeward, cried,
"In heaven we all shall meet;"—
When in the snow the mother spied
The print of Lucy's feet.

Then downwards from the steep hill's edge
They tracked the footmarks small;
And through the broken hawthorn-hedge,
And by the long stone-wall.

And then an open field they crossed,
The marks were still the same;
They tracked them on, nor ever lost,
And to the bridge they came.

They followed from the snowy bank
Those footmarks, one by one,
Into the middle of the plank:
And further there were none!

—Yet some maintain that to this day
She is a living child,

That you may see sweet Lucy Gray
Upon the lonesome wild.

O'er rough and smooth she trips along,
And never looks behind;
And sings a solitary song
That whistles in the wind.

POOR SUSAN.

At the corner of Wood Street, when daylight appears,
There's a thrush that sings loud,—it has sung for three years;
Poor Susan has passed by the spot, and has heard
In the silence of morning the song of the bird.

'Tis a note of enchantment; what ails her? She sees
A mountain ascending, a vision of trees;
Bright volumes of vapor through Lothbury glide,
And a river flows on through the vale of Cheapside.

Green pastures she views in the midst of the dale,
Down which she so often has tripped with her pail;
And a single small cottage, a nest like a dove's,
The one only dwelling on earth that she loves.

She looks, and her heart is in heaven; but they fade,—
The mist and the river, the hill and the shade:
The stream will not flow, and the hill will not rise,
And the colors all have all passed away from her eyes.

www.ingramcontent.com/pod-product-compliance
Lightning Source LLC
Chambersburg PA
CBHW021218020426
42331CB00003B/369